All About Emperor Penguins

Kerrily Sapet

EZ Readers
An imprint of Mitchell Lane Publishers

CREATING YOUNG NONFICTION READERS

EZ Readers offer nonfiction for beginning readers in PreK through first grade, using simple language, clear illustrations, and engaging facts to build vocabulary and confidence.

TIPS FOR READING NONFICTION WITH BEGINNING READERS

Talk about Nonfiction

Begin by explaining that nonfiction books give us information that is true. The book will be organized around a specific topic or idea, and we may learn new facts through reading.

Look at the Parts

Most nonfiction books have helpful features. Our *EZ Readers* include color photographs and graphic aids, a table of contents, a glossary, and an index. Share the purpose of these features with your reader.

Color Photos and Graphic Aids

A lot of information can be found by "reading" photos, charts, maps, and other graphic aids found within nonfiction texts. Help your reader learn more about the different ways information can be displayed.

Table of Contents

Located at the front of the book, this list shows the big ideas within the text and the page numbers where they can be found.

Glossary

Located at the back of the book, the glossary defines key words and phrases that are related to the topic. These words and phrases can be found in the text in colored type.

Index

Located at the back of the book, an index is an alphabetical list of topics and the page numbers where they can be found.

With a little help and guidance about reading nonfiction, you can feel good about introducing a young reader to the world of *EZ Readers* nonfiction books.

EZ Readers is an imprint of:

Mitchell Lane PUBLISHERS

2001 SW 31st Avenue
Hallandale, FL 33009
mitchelllanepub.com

First Edition, 2026.

Author: Kerrily Sapet
Editor: Morgan Brody

ISBN 979-8-89260-850-3 (library binding)
ISBN 979-8-90145-043-7 (paperback)
ISBN 979-8-89260-947-0 (ebook)

LC record available at https://lccn.loc.gov/2025950859

Photo credits: Adobe, Pixasquare, cover, 1, 2, 3, 4, 8, 12, 15,19, 21, 22, 23, 24; Adobe, Tukinoto, cover, 1; Shutterstock, Altitude Visual, cover, 1; Adobe, Zayn Arfn, 3, 9, 10, 14, 18; Shutterstock, Volodymyr TVERDOKHLIB, 5; Shutterstock, Mathias Berlin, 6–7; Shutterstock, CG Stocker, 9; Shutterstock, juan68, 10–11; Shutterstock, Myeongho Seo, 12–13, 22; Shutterstock, Timothy Yue, 14; Shutterstock, alm. And.pencil, 15, 22; Shutterstock, Altitude Visual, 18, 22; Shutterstock, vladsilver, 20, 22; Shutterstock, Alexey Seafarer, 21; Shutterstock, max dallocco, 22; Shutterstock, ValerieVSBN, 22; Shutterstock, Aouad Mokhtaria, 22

Table of Contents

Meeting an Amazing Bird 4
Penguin Watching 8
Looking for Food 15
Where Do Emperor Penguins Live? 16
Emperor Penguin Families and the Future . . 19
Parts of an Emperor Penguin 21
Glossary 22
Quiz 23
Further Reading 24
On the Internet 24
Index 24
About the Author 24

Meeting An Amazing Bird

Imagine you are in a land of snow and ice. Wind blows around you. Your warm clothes keep you safe in the freezing air.

An animal slides across the snow on its belly. It dives into the icy ocean. It is an emperor penguin! It's as tall as a second grader and weighs as much as a big dog. Emperor penguins live in **Antarctica**, the coldest, windiest place on Earth.

Penguin Watching

You see another emperor penguin. Its belly is white. Its back, head, and wings are black. Short thick feathers cover the penguin's body and legs. Yellow-gold feathers shine near its head.

PENGUIN POWER!

Penguins have layers of feathers like **armor** to protect them from the cold.

PENGUIN POWER!

Emperor penguins can dive deeper than any other bird.

The ice is slippery! Penguins have thick claws to grip the ice. They have short legs and walk slowly. Penguins flop and slide on their bellies in the snow, like riding a sled. It's faster and easier than walking.

You hear more penguins. They honk and whistle. They sound like trumpets. Penguins make noises to **communicate**. Each penguin has a special call to find its family.

PENGUIN POWER!

A penguin's black and white colors make it harder for other animals to see them in the water.

Looking for Food

More penguins splash into the cold ocean. Penguins hunt for food together. They eat fish and **squid**. Penguins have spiky tongues to hold slippery fish.

You see too many penguins to count. Penguins live in groups called **colonies**. Thousands of penguins may live together. They **huddle** together to stay warm.

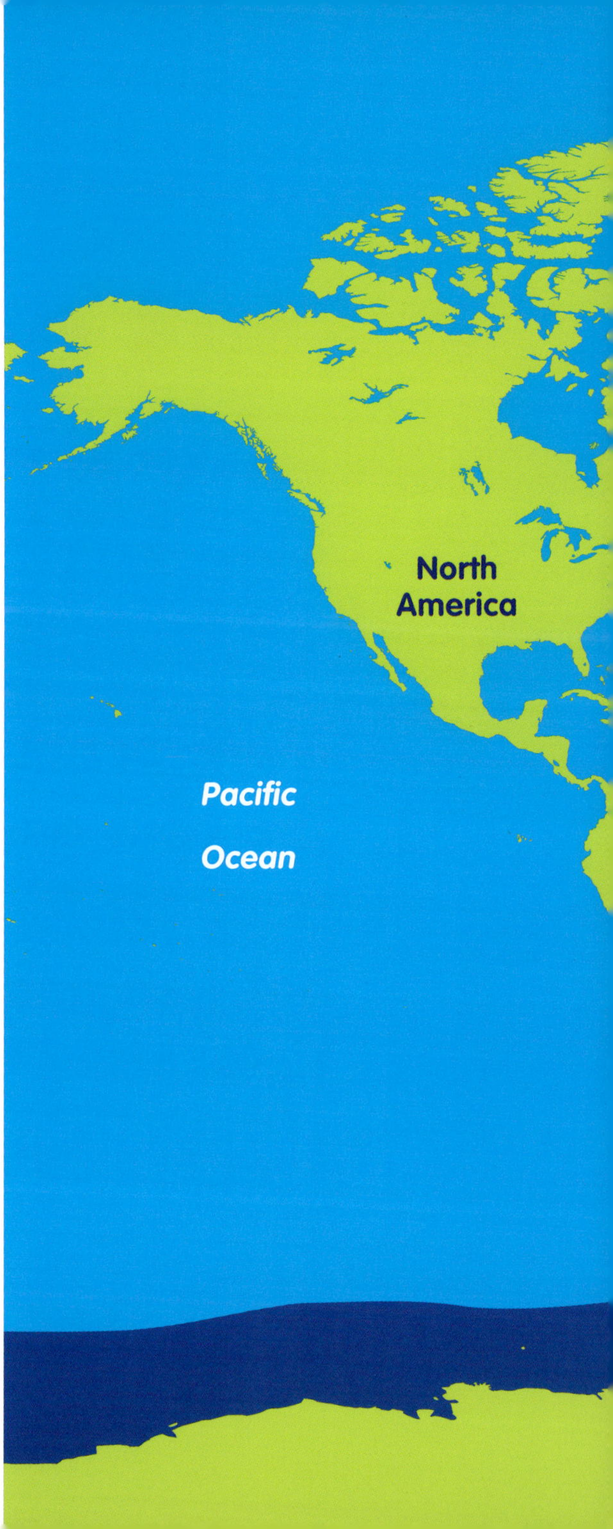

Where Do Emperor Penguins Live?

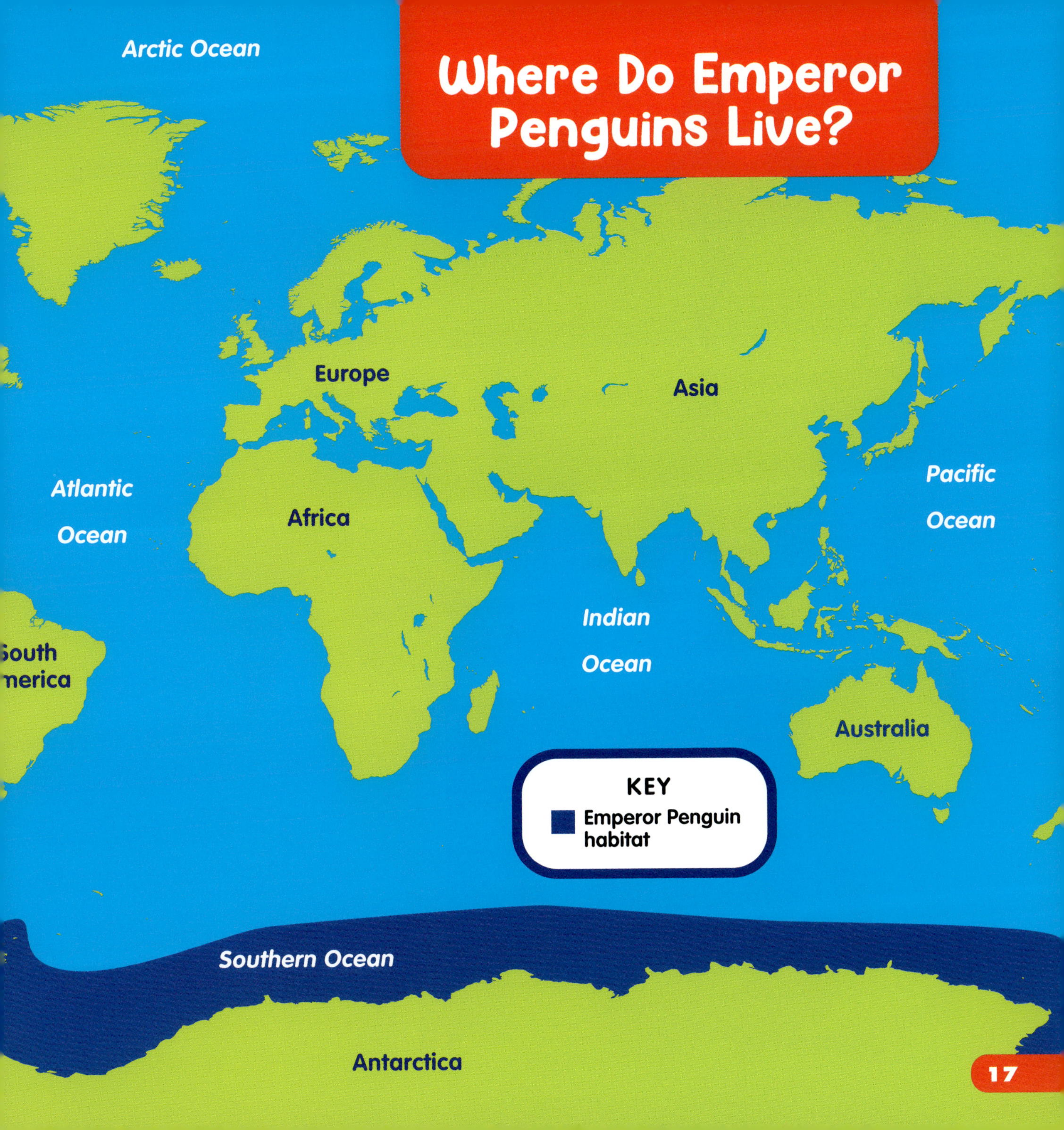

PENGUIN POWER!

An emperor penguin egg is the size of a softball.

Emperor Penguin Families and the Future

You see fluffy baby penguins called **chicks**. Chicks hatch from eggs. Fathers keep the eggs warm on their feet. Chicks are the size of bananas. Parents take turns caring for them.

Emperor penguins live 15 to 20 years. They need the snow and ice on Earth to survive. Someday you might see a real emperor penguin.

Parts of an Emperor Penguin

Eyes

Emperor penguins see well on land and underwater.

Bill

Emperor penguins have bills. A bill is a hard mouth, like a beak, that helps an animal catch and hold food.

Feathers

Emperor penguins have tiny feathers that fit tightly together to help keep them warm.

Feet

Emperor penguins have sharp claws on their two feet. Their webbed feet have skin between the toes to help them paddle in the water.

Glossary

Antarctica (ant-ARK-tik-uh) a very cold place near the bottom of the Earth where there is ice and snow

armor (ar-mor) something strong that protects the body

chick (ch-ik) a baby penguin

colony (coll-uh-nee) a group of penguins

communicate (kuh-myoon-i-kayt) to share ideas or feelings by making sounds

huddle (HUD-uhl) to stand or sit very close together

squid (sk-wid) an ocean animal with a long, soft body and ten arms

Quiz

1. Do emperor penguins live in trees?

   A. Yes B. No

2. Do penguins have warm feathers?

   A. Yes B. No

3. Do emperor penguins eat plants?

   A. Yes B. No

4. Are penguin babies called chicks?

   A. Yes B. No

ANSWER KEY:

1. No
2. Yes
3. No
4. Yes

Further Reading

DK. *Emperor Penguins.* London, England: DK Children, 2023.

Geron, Eric. *Galapagos Penguin or Emperor Penguin.* New York, NY: Children's Press, 2022.

Scheffer, Janie. *Emperor Penguins.* New York, NY: Blastoff! Readers, 2026.

On the Internet

Animals of the Ice: Emperor Penguins

https://oceantoday.noaa.gov/animalsoftheice_emperorpenguin/
Watch a video to learn more about emperor penguins.

Emperor Penguins

https://www.antarctica.gov.au/about-antarctica/animals/penguins/emperor-penguin/
Listen to penguin calls and sneezes.

Emperor Penguins

https://kids.nationalgeographic.com/animals/birds/facts/emperor-penguin
Read more and see pictures of emperor penguins.

Index

Antarctica, 7, 16–17, 22
babies, 18–19, 22
families, 12, 19
feathers, 8, 9, 19, 21
food, 15
groups, 16
size, 7, 18, 19
sounds, 12–13, 22
swim, 14

About the Author

Kerrily Sapet has written more than 40 books for kids. She lives near Chicago with her family. When she was in third grade, her uncle went to Antarctica. She loved seeing pictures and hearing stories about his trip. Sapet has never seen a real emperor penguin. She hopes to see one someday.